THE INNS AND ALEHOUSES Of YORK

by

Alan Johnson

HUTTON PRESS

1989

Published by the Hutton Press Ltd.
130 Canada Drive, Cherry Burton, Beverley
East Yorkshire HU17 7SB

*Printed by
Clifford Ward & Co. (Bridlington) Ltd.
55 West Street, Bridlington, East Yorkshire
YO15 3DZ*

ISBN 0 907033 81 4

Acknowledgements

During the process of writing this book I visited every single featured public house (and still remained sober).

The enthusiasm and assistance from, not only, all the licensees, but on a number of occasions, relief managers as well, made my research that much easier.

I am indebted to the Breweries of Bass North at Leeds, Camerons at Hartlepool, John Smiths at Tadcaster and Joshua Tetleys at Leeds for access to their own archives and to the Yorkshire Evening Press for a rummage through their Library section.

As a first time researcher I could not have got by without the help from Rita Freedman and her assistant, Mary Thallon, at the York Archives and the staff at both the York City Library and the Borthwick Institute. My thanks also to Jennifer Kaner and Hugh Murray, two respected York historians, whose own knowledge and enthusiasm encouraged me with this my first book.

Wherever possible I have obtained details from original sources and documents but acknowledge the works of the following for filling in the gaps.

Some Old York Inns	*T.P. Cooper*
Inns and Inn Signs of York	*T.P. Cooper*
Eboracum	*F. Drake*
Royal Commission on Historical Monuments	
Yorks Golden Fleece	*L. Mollett*
History of York	*C.B. Knight*
History of York	*G. Benson*
York House Books	

Contents

Introduction

The City of York, with its Minster, Bar Walls and Ancient Towers is steeped in history, from Viking and Roman settlements to medieval battles. There is, however, one other group of buildings that add as much colour and interest as their more famous counterparts — the old Inns and Alehouses.

Today we class them as either Hotels or Pubs but in days gone by the Inns, Taverns and Ale-houses each played their own distinctive role. The medieval inn is the forerunner to our modern hotel. The name is of Saxon origin meaning room, chamber or house for the lodging and entertaining of travellers.

The old inn-keeper was called an Ostler, from the French *Hostelier* and he had to maintain a certain standard and level of facilities. This, however, was not always the case, as many inns were dirty, insanitary and the base for many a criminal.

Strictly speaking the inn was not a drinking place; this role was met by the taverns and ale and beer-houses.

A Vintner was the wholesaler of wine to the Taverner who would then retail it on his premises, often frequented by the middle and upper classes. In the 16th century the licensee of a beer or ale-house was called a Tipler and later an ale-draper or ale-seller. Usually smaller than an inn or tavern, many of the old ale-houses developed into what we now refer to as the pub.

The early Kings and Queens soon realised that here was a good source of revenue from taxes, and many laws were passed governing the sale of ales and wines. Not only national laws, but also many local by-laws were made. In 1459 it was ordained that any 'alien' coming from foreign parts could only stay at the Bull in Conying Street. This inn was owned by the Lord Mayor and Commonalty of York. Failure to comply was met with a fine of 40s.

On 5th October 1477, Edward IV passed a law that no man or woman should hold a common Ostrie (hostel) without a sign over the door on penalty of 13s.4d.

Apart from the gentry, very few people could read or write, which led to most inn signs being of a pictorial nature, often designed to attract a particular type of customer or to show their allegiance to a cause or person.

During the reign of James I (1603-1625), to be found guilty of being drunk and disorderly was punishable by a fine of 5s or two hours in the stocks.

An amusing reference from the York House Book of 1613 records 'A watch to be kept at the Bars on Sundays from 8-11am and 12-3pm to prevent the meaner sort of people going to ale-houses in places adjoining the City when they should be at Church'.

During the 17th and 18th centuries the main form of public transport was by coach and, as the journey from York to London took 4 days, many new inns sprang up to cater for the weary traveller and to provide stabling for the horses. Some of the York pubs today still show evidence of the role they played during the peak coaching days.

When George Stephenson operated the first public railway journey from Stockton to Darlington in 1825 he marked the end of an era for the coaching trade and sparked off a new need for larger commercial hotels. Today the public houses within the City Walls of York are made up from a selection of the old inns, taverns, coaching houses and ale-houses — some catering for the modern, younger drinker, some for the tourist, while others still remain the traditional ale-house.

York's Oldest Pub

It is understandable that many of the pubs in York would like to lay claim to this title. The answer should be looked at in two parts.

The Oldest Licensed Premises –
The earliest reference uncovered to date is that of the Starre in Stonegate. This confirms that the Starre, in its present location, was an inn from at least 1644.

The Golden Fleece in the Pavement can be traced back to 1656 and further research may take it back even earlier.

It may well be that one or two other York inns, such as the Red Lion or the Old White Swan were indeed licensed before 1644. But without proof no claim can be made.

The Oldest Building –
This title probably comes down to one of two. The Black Swan in Peaseholme Green and the Red Lion in Merchantgate.

In his will (dated 1437) William Bowes senior refers to his capital messuage with buildings and appurtenances in Peaseholme and also three newly built tenements in Peaseholme. As the Black Swan appears to be made up from three separate buildings, could the new tenements that Bowes referred to be, in fact, the buildings that eventually became the Black Swan?

The Red Lion, however, claims to have discovered a 13th century bread oven on the premises. It is doubtful though, that the Red Lion is 200 years older than the Black Swan.

Whatever the answer, we have got two beautifully preserved buildings that both deserve a place in the history books of York.

The Inns and Ale-Houses of York

Due to the limitations of space it would not be possible to feature all the licensed premises within the City Walls so this book deals with the older and more traditional public house.

Apart from the forty pubs featured, seven other premises are mentioned here.

Two hotels that have played an important role over the years are the White Swan, which is now situated in Piccadilly, and the Railway King in George Hudson Street.

For many years the White Swan was one of York's main coaching houses. The entrance was from the Pavement before Piccadilly was built in 1912. Today the White Swan still caters for travellers as a busy city centre hotel.

The Railway King, named after the great rail pioneer George Hudson, is another busy hotel. Originally it was a Temperance hotel called the Adelphi, built in 1851. There was however, a pub on this site called the Royal Oak and later re-named the Ship as early as 1647. Although the sign in Museum Street refers to Thomas's as a hotel, accommodation is no longer available. It is built on the site of the former Etridge's or Royal Hotel as it became known. It has just undergone major refurbishment to provide more extensive catering facilities.

Meals are available from 12.00 till 2.30 and the restaurant is open on Wednesday, Thursday and Friday evenings.

Harry's Cafe Bar in Micklegate is a modern pub that caters for the younger drinker, while Walkers Bar further down Micklegate offers a variety of traditional Theakstone's ales.

The Bonding Warehouse in Skeldergate was built in 1873 to store foreign merchandise for customs. For many years Rowntrees used it to store packing material before Tetley's turned it into a pub and restaurant. Inside there are many mementoes of its warehousing days and during the summer, a catwalk, jutting out over the river, provides an idyllic setting for a quiet drink.

The Lendal Cellars is Whitbread's only public house in York and is situated on two levels in the cellars below the former house of the Oldfield family. It was opened in 1984 and the arched drinking areas have been left with all the original brickwork exposed.

The Richard III, formerly the Grob and Ducat, is situated on the corner of Rougier St. and Tanner Row. This was the Ebor Cafe from 1893 until 1974 when it became a public house. The rear part of the building is 17th century and features a fine Tudor style wooden framed fire-place. The rear wall on the Tanner Row side is of particular interest as it is built of large stone blocks and is from a much earlier construction. Offering a variety of real ales, this is one for the traditional beer tippler.

The Acorn

St. Martins Lane   Cameron's Brewery   (map ref. No.1)

Tucked away down the narrow alley of St. Martins Lane, off Micklegate, is the Acorn.

Up until 1783 the Acorn consisted of a house and yard owned by John Taylor (joyner) and his wife Ann. John Hill, who owned the nearby Golden Ball in Fetter Lane, purchased the property and turned it into a public house under the sign of the Ackhorne.

After a number of owners the Acorn was eventually purchased in 1884 by the Brewers, Hotham & Co. who subsequently became the Tadcaster Tower Brewery Company.

There must have been a tremendous amount of activity among the main Brewers when the Tower Brewery went bankrupt in 1961, and also earlier when John Kilby, who owned many public houses in York, also went bankrupt in 1819.

The Acorn was taken over by the Hartlepool Brewers, Camerons, in 1961 who were themselves acquired by Brent Walker in 1989.

The plank on which the Tap Room customers used to be served has gone and the old Smoke Room and Vaults now form one main bar area, serving a range of traditional ales, with lunch-time bar snacks and Ploughmans served every day.

The Anglers Arms

Goodramgate   John Smith's Brewery   (map ref. No.2)

Reputed to be the most haunted pub in York, the Anglers Arms certainly has the premises to support such a claim.

A very well preserved building dating from the 16th century with evidence that shows it may well have been called the Painters Arms as early as 1769 under the occupation of Edward Powell.

Edward's son John purchased the property for £100 in 1778 and it remained in the Powell family until 1841, when it went under the sign of the Square and Compass.

William Cooper then paid £360 for the property and changed the name to the Board.

It was not listed as the Anglers Arms until 1896 when Edward Staines was the licensee.

The external facade belies the wealth of medieval timbers and cosiness that lies within. The front main bar is interesting in that the first floor in one half has disappeared over the years leaving an insight to its early construction.

There is a cosy little snug to the side of the bar and a smaller room to the rear with a comforting stone fireplace.

Relax and soak up the atmosphere of this ancient little pub but keep an eye out for the pub cat, apparently playing with an unseen guest.

Bar snacks are served at lunch-time from 12.00 to 3.00 pm.

The Bar Hotel

Micklegate   Tetley Brewery   (map ref. No.3)

Although Nathaniel Early was a wine cooper in 1767, when he paid £400 for the premises, it was a further 100 years before the building became licensed premises.

For many years Robert Wilson ran his hairdressing business from here until James Wake purchased the property on 12th September 1861.

James Wake ran it as an hotel and by 1867 it was listed as the Bar Hotel. As the name suggests the Bar Hotel is situated adjacent to Micklegate Bar and at some time since 1853 a second floor was added to elevate it above the City Walls.

During its early license the Bar had two other neighbours, the Barefoot next door but one, which closed down in 1928, and the Jolly Bacchus situated across the road. This was pulled down for street widening in 1873.

Today there are no longer any guests staying here and the ground floor has been opened out into one main bar area with a small snug to the side. Both hot and cold snacks are served at lunch-time while at night it reverts to a popular drinking place.

The Black Swan

Peaseholme Green   Bass Brewery   (map ref. No.4)

The Black Swan is one of the best preserved and picturesque inns in York. Dating back to the 14th century, it was once an extremely fine country residence, providing home to many a notable family.

One such family were the Bowes, who owned the property for many generations. Sir Martin Bowes, who

To the rear is another smaller room that boasts a secret escape hole above another large fireplace. It is believed that cock fighting took place in a room above.

Climbing the wide, creaking oak staircase one could quite expect to be greeted by Henry himself, as a sense of history engulfs all who enter the large functions room at the top.

The oak panelling around this room features faded pictures painted directly onto the panels and a fireplace tiled with rare blue and white Delph tiles.

Bed and Breakfast accommodation is available as well as lunch-time bar meals. Private parties for business or social events can be catered for in one of a number of old rooms.

The Blue Bell

Fossgate   John Smith's Brewery   (map ref. No.5)

The expression 'time stood still' is the only way to describe York's smallest public house.

Consisting of just one small bar area to the front and a small snug, the price of a pint is still rung up on an old £.s.d. till with the licensee popping out from a curtain at the back of the bar.

There was another and much older Blue Bell in Fossgate which once stood on the corner with Hosier Lane, now the Pavement.

spent a happy childhood here, became a respected London goldsmith and was elected Lord Mayor of London in 1545 during the reign of Henry VIII

Stepping past the solid-oak front door, with its original peephole, is like stepping back to medieval days. The oak-panelled front room features an old oil painting, framed into the panels, that looks as old as the building itself.

The Ingle bar abounds with items and artefacts of bygone days. The main feature of this room is the large open fireplace, complete with roasting spit, just waiting for the 'Ox' to be turned.

Being in the same street and in the same parish leads to some confusion when tracing the history of the present Blue Bell, but the change took place sometime between 1782 and 1851.

On January 9th 1902 George Robinson took out the license for the Blue Bell and it has remained in the family ever since.

George was one of the first Directors of York City Football Club and some of the early private meetings were held at the Blue Bell prior to the official forming of the Club in 1922.

When George died, his wife Annie Robinson took over the license to be followed by their daughter Edith Pinder, who at the time of writing is still the licensee.

A serious fire in May 1974 nearly destroyed this unique little pub but fortunately the damage was repaired without changing its character. It is a centrally situated pub that has closed its eye to all the changes around it.

The Boulevard

Stonebow   Bass Brewery   (map ref. No. 7)

Standing on the corner of Fossgate and Stonebow, opposite the site of the ancient church of St. Crux, is the recently refurbished Boulevard. One of York's larger public houses, it was once a wine and spirit vaults owned

by a Mr. Wilson, who in 1899 paid £1,200 for it.

Up until 1956 it was known as the 'Board' when it was renamed the 'Stonebow' after the new road of the same name was built, taking part of the original building with it.

The Boulevard is situated on the site of a medieval Carmelite Friary which moved within the city walls in 1295.

Stonebow Lane, which is derived from the word *staynebowe*, meaning stone arch, ran along side the Northern wall of the Friary and was referred to as White Friar Lane in 1471.

The recent refurbishment of the Boulevard has produced a balanced Victorian atmosphere with stained-glass windows, brass-ware and life-sized porcelain replicas of wild animals, representing trophies from the heady Empire days of Queen Victoria.

A raised area at one end of the large, open bar caters for the ever-increasing lunch-time trade with an interesting variety of home-cooked specialities.

The Brewers Arms

Tanner Row   Tetley Brewery   (map ref. No.8)

When Newsam and Gott of Leeds surveyed the Brewers Arms for Joshua Tetley in 1899 they reported that the trade was mainly 'pint pot trade'. Although the price of $1\frac{3}{4}$d. a pint has changed a little, the role of the Brewers Arms is still that of a drinking man's pub.

The whole area around this site is currently undergoing a lot of changes and it may well be that the Brewers Arms has to change accordingly. It was once a lot smaller with an adjoining shop and a small cottage to the rear.

These two buildings boosted the owner's income by 6/- per week from the shop and 3s.9d. a week from the cottage.

The original bar still remains but a newer lounge has now replaced both the shop and the cottage.

At the time of writing there were no cooking facilities on the premises, but this may change in the near future.

The Brown Cow

Hope St.   Timothy Taylor's   (map ref. No.9)

The Brown Cow is a typical 'local', the *Rovers Return* of Hope St. situated well away from the city centre and with no fancy gimmicks to attract customers or spoil its appearance.

Following major housing developments in this area in the 1930's, the Brown Cow survived the bulldozer and continues to serve the local community.

Apart from a small lounge area the main accent is on the traditional pub games of darts, dominoes and pool.

The Brown Cow claims to have hosted a darts match, broadcast live on radio back in 1939, when it boasted six dart boards.

Things haven't changed much over the years as the regulars have raised over £3000 for charity from pool and domino marathons.

It is Timothy Taylor's only public house in York and offers a range of traditional beers.

The Coach

Micklegate   Tetley Brewery   (map ref. No.10)

The Coach in Micklegate, formerly the Coach and Horses, used to be referred to as the 'Little Coach' in comparison to the 'Big Coach' which was situated in Nessgate and is no longer there.

It consists of two separate dwellings: the original Coach and Horses which is the southern part of the building was bought at public auction by Joshua Tetley in 1945; and the premises next door were purchased the following year.

Up until 1854 the archway of the former Benedictine, Trinity Priory stood alongside the latter building. When this archway, together with a number of other tenements were demolished, the new Priory Street was formed. Prior to 1945, the Coach was for 30 years vested in the Official Trustees of Charity Lands (known as Richard Pickard's Charity).

The two buildings now form one long bar area, decorated in light coloured woods and modern brassware, with bar meals served every lunch-time.

The Cock and Bottle

Skeldergate   John Smith's Brewery   (map ref. No.11)

The present Cock and Bottle is a relatively new building but its links with the past can rival many of York's older ale-houses.

There is some evidence, when Skeldergate was a main thoroughfare serving the wharfes along the banks of the Ouse, that a house existed here as early as 1575.

This house would have been in the grounds of a splendid residence which was built by Lord Thomas Fairfax at the beginning of the 17th century. When Lord Fairfax died in 1671 his residence and grounds went to his daughter Mary and her husband George Villiers, 'Duke of Buckingham'. The Duke was a notorious ladies' man and was eventually banished from the Royal Court, returning to York "worn to a thread by whoring".

Along with his demise came increasing debts and this lovely residence, now known as Duke's Place, began to crumble around him. Some believe that his ghost still frequents the area, mourning his misfortunes.

After a number of alterations and additions, the original dwelling became a beer house known as the Plumbers Arms around 1875 and was purchased by John Smith's Tadcaster Brewery Company in 1909.

They fought a hard battle to retain and preserve the building until 1962 when the Corporation decided, in the name of progress, that the widening of Skeldergate was more important than the preservation of this and many other old buildings.

Today the Cock and Bottle, meaning draught and bottled beers, has retained many of the original features and fittings from the old Plumbers Arms, resulting in a modern pub with a genuine old-world feel to it.

Bar meals are available at lunch-time with a variety of entertainment in the evenings, including occasional special events such as Christmas parties in June.

The Corner Pin

Tanner Row
John Smith's Brewery
(map ref. No.12)

Up until 1985 the Corner Pin went under the sign of the 'Unicorn' and is now known as the Corner Pin Carvery.

Although the name may have changed the older part of the pub certainly hasn't. The charming front bar, with its leaded windows and old wooden bench seats, has not altered much over the years.

A recent addition to the building is a conservatory-style restaurant which somehow manages to blend in quite well with the older part of the building.

The licensee has also managed to achieve the art of providing excellent dining facilities while at the same time maintaining a true drinking pub atmosphere in the bar and cosy back-room.

The daily menu consists of a choice of roasts from the carvery or a selection from the *à la carte* menu on Thursday, Friday and Saturday evenings up until 10.00 pm.

The Cross Keys

Goodramgate
Bass Brewery
(map ref. No.13)

The original Cross Keys, which stood on the same site, dated back hundreds of years and was completely rebuilt at the beginning of this century.

The sign of the Cross Keys is associated with the apostle Peter. It was once owned by the church and was purchased by James Melrose in 1888 from Reverend Arthur Percival representing the Dean Purey Cust.

The rebuilding would have coincided with the construction of the new Deangate in 1902, when part of the original site was sold to the Corporation.

Triangular shaped, due to its corner position, one side of the central bar area caters for lunch-time diners, while a kitchen theme is maintained at the other side in the lounge area.

The Cross Keys is centrally situated and offers accommodation with views of the Minster as well as providing a variety of home-cooked meals every lunch-time; including a traditional value-for-money Roast Beef and Yorkshire Pudding on Sundays.

The Falcon

Micklegate   John Smith's Brewery   (map ref. No.14)

The Falcon is one of York's oldest Inns and has provided a high class of accommodation for at least 245 years. The York *Courant* of 1743 stated that the Falcon in Micklegate was to be auctioned on November 22nd when the licensee was Joseph Anderea.

On April 24th 1756, when John Shepherd was the licensee, Lt. Col. Bucks had five of his soldiers billeted here. Just over 100 years later the licensee J. Harrison was not so lucky, as Robert Dawson robbed him of two flannel shirts.

The Falcon's longest-serving landlord was George Smithson who lasted from at least 1765 to 1798.

Running from No. 94 Micklegate through to Tanner Row at the rear, where the stables once stood, the number 70 on the back door did not refer to 70 Tanner Row but was the old number in Micklegate before a re-numbering scheme in 1913.

Apart from a few minor alterations the building is very much as it was hundreds of years ago.

Accommodation is available throughout the year with lunch-time meals served seven days a week.

The Five Lions

Walmgate   Bass Brewery   (map ref. No.15)

Documentary evidence shows than an earlier dwelling on this site was referred to as the City Arms and was mortgaged on 5th May 1702 for £120. Around the turn of the 18th century it was rebuilt to cater for the increasing stage and coaching trade, evidence of which can still be seen from the extensive stabling in the rear yard.

The sign of the Five Lions, which forms the City of York's coat of arms, used to have inscribed below it "vino bono non opus est hedera" (good wines need no bush), which meant good wines needed no advertising. The 'bush' is of Roman origin and represents one of the earliest recorded inn signs.

The present Five Lions was refurbished in 1981 and features a fine long-panelled bar and beamed ceilings, with only a small section of stained glass remaining of its earlier construction.

Conveniently situated close to the City centre, home-cooked luncheons are available through the week and larger parties can be catered for on request.

The Golden Ball

Cromwell Rd.   John Smith's Brewery   (map ref. No.16)

Today the Golden Ball is situated on the corner of Victor St. (formerly St. Mary's Row) and Cromwell Rd. (formerly Jail Lane) in the Parish of St. Mary's Bishophill senior.

The name changes of the two roads together with the fact that there was another Golden Ball in Fetter Lane in the Parish of St. Mary's Bishophill junior led to a considerable amount of confusion when tracing the history of this public house.

Jail Lane, a narrow thoroughfare, was so named because it linked the City with the former Ancient Prison of the Archbishops of York, which was situated behind Baile Hill.

The Golden Ball with its red-faced brickwork is of Victorian style both inside and out, not a reproduced effect but all original. The Monarchy, and latterly the Governments, of our country have managed to tax just about every conceivable item over the years; from the number of windows and fires, to bricks and the number of rooms. The Golden Ball still retains the old numbers on all the different rooms including the cellar.

It is a Victorian local, just off the main stream tourist track, that has escaped the ravages of modernisation.

The Golden Fleece

Pavement   Bass Brewery   (map ref. No.17)

The Golden Fleece, situated in the Pavement, is another inn that could well prove to be the oldest licensed premises in York.

The inn sign comes from the commercial importance that the wool trade gave York, which by 1377 was second only to London.

During the turbulent reign of Charles II (1660-1685), a number of York merchants were allowed to mint their own copper half-pennies and the figure below shows that of Richard Booth at the Golden Fleece, probably dated around 1667.

The Fleece, as it was often referred to, later became a major coaching inn with the stabling situated in the yard at the rear. This yard is named after Lady Alice Peckett, wife of John Peckett, who was the Lord Mayor of York in 1702 and who owned the Fleece at that time.

As one of York's ancient high class inns, many licensees have taken out their Freedom of the Company of Innholders while serving here, people like Christopher Smithies in 1787 and William Clark in 1794.

The narrow entrance in the Pavement opens out into a large lounge to the rear down a long timber-framed passage.

The lack of foundations to the building adds to the quaintness of this old pub, that offers accommodation as well as serving home-cooked meals from 12.00 till 10.00pm. Most of the bedrooms, in keeping with the period of the pub, have four-poster beds, including the Honeymoon suite.

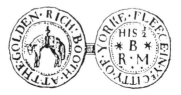

The Golden Lion

Church St.
Grand Metropolitan
(map ref. No.18)

Due to the poor state of the building in 1971, the old Golden Lion was demolished and completely rebuilt, taking on the new name of the 'Nineteen Hundred', which was to commemorate the founding of York in AD71. The license of the original building can be traced back to 1711 when Thomas Hessay took out the lease from Abraham Goodgione for £71.1s.6d; the property was described as a warehouse.

Thomas Hessay subsequently bought the property by borrowing the money from Richard Booth of the Golden Fleece and turned it into a public house under the sign of the Golden Lion.

Key to map

1.	Acorn	St. Martins Lane
2.	Anglers Arms	Goodramgate
3.	Bar Hotel	Micklegate
4.	Black Swan	Peaseholme Green
5.	Blue Bell	Fossgate
6.	Bonding Warehouse	Skeldergate
7.	Boulevard	Stonebow
8.	Brewers Arms	Tanner Row
9.	Brown Cow	Hope Street
10.	Coach	Micklegate
11.	Cock and Bottle	Skeldergate
12.	Corner Pin	Tanner Row
13.	Cross Keys	Goodramgate
14.	Falcon	Micklegate
15.	Five Lions	Walmgate
16.	Golden Ball	Bishophill
17.	Golden Fleece	Pavement
18.	Golden Lion	Church Street
19.	Golden Slipper	Goodramgate
20.	Grapes	King Street
21.	Great Northern	Hudson Street
22.	Hansom Cab	Market Street
23.	Harry's Cafe Bar	Micklegate
24.	Hole in the Wall	High Petergate
25.	Kings Arms	Kings Staith
26.	Lendal Bridge	Tanners Moat
27.	Lendal Cellars	St. Helens Square
28.	Little John	Castlegate
29.	Lowther	Kings Staith
30.	Nags Head	Micklegate
31.	Old White Swan	Goodramgate
32.	Phoenix	George Street
33.	Punch Bowl	Stonegate
34.	Railway King	Hudson Street
35.	Red Lion	Merchantgate
36.	Richard III	Rougier Street
37.	Roman Bath	St. Sampsons Square
38.	Royal Oak	Goodramgate
39.	Spread Eagle	Walmgate
40.	Thomas's Hotel	Museum Street
41.	Three Cranes	St. Sampsons Square
42.	Three Tuns	Coppergate
43.	Walkers Bar	Micklegate
44.	White Swan	Piccadilly
45.	William Bass	Market Street
46.	Ye Olde Starre Inne	Stonegate
47.	York Arms	High Petergate
48.	Yorkshire Hussar	North Street

Up until 1836, what is now Church St. was called *Girdlergate* and provided one of the four access points into Thursday Market (St. Sampsons Sq.).

During the late 18th and early 19th century, York certainly wasn't undergoing the property price boom of modern day. In 1773 Joseph Mollett purchased the property from Ann Busfield for £715 and at a public auction held at the Red Lion, Monk Bar, on 6th May 1828, Thomas and James Bell had only to raise £710 to secure the Golden Lion.

After recent refurbishments, the 1900 returned back to the sign of the Golden Lion in 1983.

The one large open-bar area now serves lunches through the week, with weekend catering during the Summer season.

The Golden Slipper

Goodramgate   John Smith's Brewery   (map ref. No.19)

Consisting of two separate buildings, it is only possible to trace the Golden Slipper back to 1821 when Mary Marsh was the licensee.

The northern part of the pub is certainly a lot older than that and it may have been called the *Shou* prior to that date.

Although the Royal Oak is situated next door the relationship between the two buildings is much more

intimate than just neighbours, as the two buildings overlap each other at different levels.

In the older part of the Golden Slipper, evidence can clearly be seen of a passage that would have served both buildings, making the original bar of the Golden Slipper very small indeed.

A very interesting pub with plenty of exposed timbers that may well have been an ale house for a lot longer than can be traced.

The origin of the name of this pub is believed, by some, to come from a greyhound of that name and although an old shoe, found during refurbishments, is displayed in the bar the writer believes the name is the up-marketing of the old '*Shou*'.

The Grapes

King St.   Bass Brewery   (map ref. No.20)

From medieval times up until the latter half of the 19th century the area around the Grapes was known as the notorious Water Lanes, an artery of three narrow lanes connecting York's main 'dockland' of Kings Staith with the City Centre.

It was an area riddled with crime, prostitution and poverty that would have put the world's leading red-light districts to shame.

A major clearance of the area started with the widening of First Water Lane in 1852 and renaming it King St. It was at this time that the Grapes was rebuilt and took its present name after being under the sign of the Black Boy for many centuries.

The Grapes was a lodging house for professional travellers for many years after 1852. Evidence of this can be seen from a well-faded engraving on one of the front windows.

On the same window engraved 'Professional House' there is also a small and rather amusing cartoon etched in one corner, with the inscription 'Mistaken Identity'.

Today the Grapes caters for the tourist during the day offering pub lunches 7 days a week, while at night it is well supported by numerous darts and domino teams.

The Great Northern

George Hudson St.
John Smith's Brewery
(map ref. No.21)

The Great Northern was built at the same time that the York and North Midland Railway Co. built a new road connecting Micklegate to the new Railway Station in Toft Green in 1843. It was a large Commercial Hotel, catering for the influx of rail travellers as well as railway company staff.

After the Railway Station was repositioned outside the City Walls in 1877, the Great Northern continued as a hotel up until the early 1960's. The top floor was then removed and it was renamed the Pageant. Following some minor alterations in 1984 the name was changed back to the Great Northern.

It is one of York's larger public houses, but no longer taking guests, and one of the few pubs that has live entertainment with a 50's and 60's theme every Tuesday night, while Thursday evening is for the Country and Western fans.

Bar meals are served 7 days a week at lunch-time with evening meals Monday to Thursday.

The Hansom Cab

Market St.   Samuel Smith's Brewery   (map ref. No.22)

A new wide street connecting the two markets of Thursday in St. Sampsons Square and the market in the Pavement was called Parliament St. and opened on 16th June 1836 to provide further market space. This new road cut the narrow Jubbergate in two and around 1840 the Burns Hotel, the former name of the Hansom Cab, started operating as a small family-run hotel in the southern part of Jubbergate.

From 1852 onwards this part of Jubbergate was renamed Market St. The York City and County Bank was situated on the corner of Market St. and Parliament St. and it would appear that around 1870 the bank was enlarged, taking the original Burns with it.

A new Burns Hotel emerged next door to what is now the Midland Bank and was only renamed the Hansom Cab when it re-opened after refurbishment in 1985.

Like many other city-centre pubs, during the day the Hansom Cab caters for York's tourists and shoppers with a constantly varying menu of home-cooked meals, while at night it is one of the city's busiest pubs.

29

The Hole in the Wall

High Petergate   Mansfield's Inns   (map ref. No.24)

The origin of the name of this public house is the perpetual talking point among its regulars. Evidence of a debtors' prison have been found in the cellar and some claim that the prisoners were fed through a 'hole in the wall'. Others believe that the 'hole' was an escape route into the adjoining lane, possibly used by the men of the church having a sly tipple.

Formerly known as the 'Board' it is situated close to one of the ancient entrances to the city and may well claim either of the above.

In 1979 the 18th century 'Board' was in fear of collapse and it was decided to completely rebuild it using as much of the original materials as possible.

The result is a modern pub which has retained, possibly even enhanced, its old world charm, with log fires, brick walls and beamed ceilings. It was also discovered, during the rebuilding, that there is a stream running right underneath the property.

Hot and cold lunches are served midday and also Monday to Thursday evening during the high season.

The Kings Arms

Kings Staith   Samuel Smith's Brewery
(map ref. No.25)

Situated on York's oldest and, for many generations, its busiest Quay, the Kings Arms is also the oldest remaining building on Kings Staith. The first reference to it being a public house was in 1783 when James Anderson was the licensee and it is thought to have been the old customs house prior to this.

A delightful building of stone and timber framing, it also lays claim to being the most flooded pub in York.

The original doorway led directly on to the Staith at the front but was later moved to the side in King St. to allow customers access during the floods.

In 1867, during the occupation of George Duckitt, the name was changed to the Ouse Bridge Inn and remained so until it reverted back to the Kings Arms in 1974.

Because of the constant problem of flooding the cellars are situated upstairs in a room where it is believed the bodies of criminals, hung off Ouse Bridge, were laid out.

All the original supporting timbers and stone-slab floor give the relatively small L-shaped bar a real sense of history, and to cater for the increase in summer trade, tables and bench seats are located outside on the Staith.

Bar meals are served every lunch-time with meals running through to 7.00pm during the summer.

The Lendal Bridge

Tanners Moat   Bass Brewery   (map ref. No.26)

The Lendal Bridge is one of York's cosy little pubs with just one bar area and a small snug to the front; a pub that has seen many changes over the years with still more to come.

When the new Railway Station opened in Toft Green on June 4th 1841 the inadequately narrow North Street and Tanners Moat formed the main access for passengers.

It would appear that the Lendal Bridge, which was then called the Railway Tavern, first became a public house around the same time.

The York and North Midland Railway Company, under the leadership of George Hudson, agreed to build a new road connecting Micklegate and the Station. The York City Commissioners paid £1,000 towards the costs and named it Hudson Street.

It took two attempts to build Lendal Bridge (the river crossing) and it was finally opened on 8th June 1863 at a cost to the city of £35,000. The Railway Tavern subsequently changed its name to the Lendal Bridge Inn around 1884.

Today this little pub is once again in the midst of yet more changes with a new development being constructed next door.

Apart from the cosy atmosphere, hot and cold bar snacks are served at lunch-time.

The Little John

Castlegate   Grand Metropolitan   (map Ref. No.28)

Up until the late 19th century the Little John was called the Robin Hood and for many years after the change a rhyme under the new sign read 'Robin Hood is dead and gone, now come and drink with Little John'.

The existing building was built around 1730 and was designed specifically as a coaching inn, with William Flower tending such coaches as the 'Providence' which left the Robin Hood to catch the Hull Packet every morning at 7.00am, and the 'Antelope' which left daily at 11.30am for Leeds.

Not long after its construction the guests at the Robin Hood would have witnessed one of York's historic moments, when the hanged body of John Palmer, alias Dick Turpin, was brought to the nearby Blue Boar on 10th April 1739.

Almost 100 years later the Robin Hood had its own scoundrel in the form of John J. Anderson. In 1838 he was declared bankrupt after being the licensee for a number of years at the Inn. He owed £2,500 and by the following year had borrowed more money and taken up residence at the Starre in Stonegate, posing as its owner. He was eventually imprisoned for 6 months.

Before the construction of Clifford Street in 1881, Castlegate, although narrow by today's standards, was the main thoroughfare leading to the Castle and the road out to Selby.

The external view of the Little John is much as it was in 1730, but the interior has altered greatly. Modern red and green furnishings line the long bar situated on different levels, with home cooked meals served every lunch-time from 12.00 till 2.00pm.

The Lowther

Kings Staith   John Smith's Brewery   (map ref. No.29)

Following the earlier widening of First Water Lane in 1852 the York Corporation set about ridding the city of the rest of the notorious Water Lanes, including the construction of Clifford Street. This was completed in 1881 when the Lowther Hotel was built on the corner of the new Cumberland St. (formerly Middle Water Lane) and Kings Staith.

Although the Hotel part was dropped from the name in 1978, accommodation is still available with many rooms overlooking the river.

Like its neighbour, the Kings Arms, the Lowther has had its own problems with flooding, resulting in the ground floor set several feet above the level of the Staith.

During the 17th and 18th centuries there was a public washing area at the South East end of the Staith known as the *Pudding Holes*.

There have been many internal alterations since James Booth started the license in 1883, the latest being in 1986 when the present nautical theme was adopted.

There is a small front bar decorated with ships' lamps and other nautical knick-knacks and a lounge bar running through to the back.

A forty-seater restaurant on the first floor serves

guests as well as offering fine views of the river. Meals are served from 12.00 noon through to 8.30pm, either in the bar or the restaurant upstairs.

The Nags Head

Micklegate   Bass Brewery   (map ref. No.30)

The Nags Head in Micklegate, which runs right through to Toft Green at the rear, is another of York's old coaching inns.

It was, however, an inn long before the height of the coaching trade, with the license probably going back to the 16th century.

The former owners of the property, the Wesleyan Trust Property, decided to put it up for public auction on 27th June 1856 and it was subsequently sold to Thomas Kirk for £600.

The original building is 16th century but it would appear to have been rebuilt during the 18th century to cater for coach travellers and to provide stabling for horses at the rear.

Although the interior has undergone a number of changes the external facade has changed little over the years.

Situated on what is known locally as the 'Micklegate Run', the Nags Head is one of York's busiest pubs.

Lunch-time bar meals are served 5 days a week from 12.00 to 2.00pm.

The Old White Swan

Goodramgate   Bass Brewery   (map ref. No.31)

The Old White Swan is another inn that can lay claim to being one of York's oldest surviving pubs: a complex of at least nine separate buildings that is on record of being an inn as early as 1703 during the reign of Queen Anne, the last of the Stuarts.

A pigsty, barber's shop, church land, coaching house, poultry market; these are just some of the many activities that the Old White Swan has hosted over the years.

In 1983, Bass Brewery spent £3/4 million on a spectacular refurbishment which uncovered many unexpected features and gained them a well-deserved architectural award. It is a deceptively large public house with a wealth of history in every room. The front panelled lounge, complete with log fire, is reminiscent of a posh gentleman's club. To the rear is a brick-walled bar area featuring a large open fireplace that was only discovered during the refurbishments. The Gallery and Minstrel bar shows off fine examples of medieval timber framework, a hay loft, an old Yorkshire fireplace and an early sign which advertises fresh hay, a wheelwright and an Inn that is favoured by the gentry.

The old barber's shop now forms a large lounge area where children are admitted.

Accommodation is available and there is a variety of home-cooked meals at lunch-time, as well as a variety of ghosts!

The Phoenix

George Street
John Smith's Brewery
(map ref. No.32)

Tucked under the City Walls alongside Fishergate Bar, the Phoenix was called the 'Labour in Vain' up until the middle of the 19th century.

Its present name is likely to have come from the Phoenix Iron Foundry that used to be situated at the back of Fishergate Postern.

The archway to the left of the building is now blocked off to form toilets, but was originally the entrance to Eberneezer Place. This was a small courtyard that had twelve houses surrounding it.

This superb little pub is immaculately decorated both inside and out and it is easy to understand why the front bar was used as a T.V. set in 1973 for a play called 'Days of Hope' which was set in 1916.

Like the front bar, the U-shaped lounge to the rear has kept its period atmosphere, complete with piano for a traditional Sunday night sing-song.

Home cooked bar meals are served at lunch-times.

The Punch Bowl

Stonegate   Bass Brewery   (map ref. No.33)

The overhanging gabled frontage of today's Punch Bowl along with some of the timber panelling and beams within are the result of a major refurbishment in 1931. The pub however is another of York's oldest inns that has offered accommodation for many hundreds of years.

A Captain Montgomery had his sergeant Dowlin and another soldier billeted here in 1756, when the licensee was Francis Chaddock.

In 1765 the old Tenor Bell Clapper from York Minster was purchased for £3.7s.6d. and now forms part of the fixtures in the rear lounge.

The sign of the Punch Bowl is of 17th century political origin. While the Tories drank sack and claret, the Whigs preferred their punch, which was a sweetened mixture of drinks.

When Frank Hoad took over the license in 1975 he started a tradition that is still kept up today. The area just in front of the main bar he designated the Old Codgers' Corner and although Frank Hoad has gone the Old Codgers are still there. It is a delightful pub with a fine collection of old York photographs adorning the panelled walls.

Accommodation is available with lunch-time meals served every day.

The Red Lion

Merchantgate   John Smith's Brewery   (map ref. No.35)

Up until 1912 the Red Lion was set back off Walmgate, tucked in behind the former Black Horse public house. Both pubs were situated next to the old pig market just above Foss Bridge.

When Piccadilly was completed, connecting Parliament St. with Fishergate Postern, a link was made through to Walmgate and named Merchantgate.

Possibly due to a name change early in the 19th century it is difficult to trace the license of the Red Lion back beyond that date.

The building, however, can rival any of York's older structures. With 13th century foundation stones, the medieval timber-framed building is in a beautiful state of preservation both inside and out.

In 1976, when Mike Casey was the licensee, what is thought to be a 13th century bread oven was discovered and now forms an interesting addition to the front bar.

On the first floor there is a priest hole between two bedrooms that had access out to the chimney. Because of its history it is understandable that many a tale has developed, including the belief that the notorious highwayman, Dick Turpin, once escaped from an upstairs window. The interior is a historian's delight with only the minimum of structural alterations to leave a true glimpse of days gone by.

Meals are served at lunch-time 7 days a week with evening meals on Thursday, Friday and Saturday. The best-seller is their own Lion sized rump steaks.

The Roman Bath

St. Sampsons Square   John Smith's Brewery
(map ref. No.37)

The Roman Bath is another pub that has had a number of name changes over the years. In 1783 when James Woodall was the licensee it was referred to as the Barrell Churn. By 1788 it had become the Cooper and then the Barrel in 1818. By 1838 the name had changed to the Mail Coach, when it played an important role during the height of York's coaching days.

In 1930, during enlargements and rebuilding, the remains of a Roman Bath were discovered under the pub some 15 feet below the present street level. During more recent refurbishments a viewing panel was built into the floor allowing the customers to be able to see the remains.

It is believed that the well preserved semi-circular bath, because of its location and size, was more likely to have belonged to a private residence rather than a public bath.

Tiles were discovered with footprint indentations as well as the markings of the 9th Legion who occupied York in AD79. Evidence exists that the later 6th Legion also had a hand in its construction in the 3rd century.

There are steps at both ends of the bath and a smaller plunge pool was found a short distance away.

One of York's older ale houses with an even older asset, centrally situated with bar-meals served every lunch-time.

The Royal Oak

Goodramgate   Cameron's Brewery   (map ref. No.38)

The Royal Oak is another of York's old ale-houses with lots of character. The license can be traced back to 1783 when Charles Popplewell was in occupation under the sign of the Blue Pigg.

When John Furness took over the license on 15th May 1794 he changed the name to the Blue Bore (sic) and it came into the ownership of John Kilby (Brewer) in 1797.

Following the bankruptcy of John Kilby in 1819 the Blue Boar was put up for public auction at the Robin Hood in Castlegate on 31st August 1819. The bidding started at £400 and eventually reached £460 from Thomas Belt who immediately changed the name to the Royal Oak.

The property eventually came into the hands of John J. Hunt in 1894, then Cameron's Brewery at Hartlepool, who are now owned by the Brent Walker Company.

The Elizabethan style brick and timber fronts two cosy rooms presided over by Dave Smith, a former landlord of the Starre in Stonegate. Dave's prowess as a big-game hunter is well documented when on the 15th

December 1984 he bagged $\frac{1}{3}$ of a share of a Crow.

Today the Royal Oak is building quite a reputation for its home-cooked meals which are served from 11.30 to 7.30 throughout the week plus Saturday and Sunday lunch-times.

The Spread Eagle

Walmgate   Free House   (map ref. No.39)

In 1800 there were no less than 26 public houses in Walmgate. The Spread Eagle is now one of only two that still remain. In 1867 William Foster, a flour dealer, was resident here before Mrs E. Dalton became the first licensee of the Spread Eagle.

William Jordan took over the license in 1909 and it remained in the Jordan family until Aloysius Jordan left in 1955. It is typical of the small ale houses that existed at the height of Walmgate's peak tippling days.

The front bar area, with its red-tiled floor, iron fireplace and old wooden corner-seat has not altered much since the turn of the century. Both this room and the snug to the rear feature a varied collection of old enamelled advertising signs, adding to the period of the pub. Although the sign outside advertises that it is a Timothy Taylor public house it is a free house that serves a variety of traditional real ales. At lunch-time home cooked meals are available all week.

The Three Cranes

St. Sampsons Square   Bass Brewery   (map ref. No.41)

Although the sign outside the Three Cranes shows three of the feathered variety, the original name is more likely to have come from the three lifting cranes that were used for loading and unloading wares and were situated to the rear of the pub, down the narrow Three Cranes Lane.

Its relatively modern facade belies the fact that this is one of York's older pubs, as the early records show that Thomas Heckford was the licensee here in 1749.

St. Sampsons Sq. was called Thursday Market up until 1818 and is one of York's oldest market places with the earliest references being made in 1250.

In 1592 the Lord Mayor of York, Thomas Harrison, ordered that linen should be sold on a Friday in Thursday Market and that a yard measure had to be kept in the Cross.

The Cross, which was erected in the centre of Thursday Market in 1429, was replaced by the Market Hall and was demolished in 1815.

To this day, the Three Cranes is still a market tavern: a plain and simple ale-house, that must have seen many generations of market traders tippling after a long day at their stalls.

The Three Tuns

Coppergate   John Smith's   (map ref. No.42)

Beer was stored in casks of different sizes: a Firkin held 9 gallons, a Kilderkin 18 gallons, a Barrel 36 gallons, a Hogshead 54 gallons and the largest was a Tun which held 216 imperial gallons of beer.

The sign of the Three Tuns is derived from the old Vintners' Coat of Arms which had a sable and chevron enarched between three tuns.

The license under the sign of the Three Tuns goes back at least to 1782 when Thomas Spink was in occupation. During the hundred years between 1830 and 1930 the name was changed to the Yorkshireman Coffee House, and then just the Yorkshireman.

There are some odd references to both the Three Tuns and the Yorkshireman being situated in Coppergate at the same time, but they refer to the same premises.

The Three Tuns is a very picturesque and unusual shaped building with a number of old supporting timbers in the front bar area. Along the right-hand side of the interior is the remains of some earlier construction in large stone blocks.

A delightful little pub that offers meals every lunchtime.

The William Bass

Market St.   Bass Brewery   (map ref. No.45)

The William Bass was, up until 1988, called the Tiger and became a licensed premises under John Burrill in 1851.

The name was changed to honour William Bass who founded the Bass Brewery in 1777 at Burton on Trent. Charrington Brewery, which was founded in 1750, joined the Bass group in 1960.

It was William Bass who took out the first registered trade mark for the famous 'red triangle' on their Red Label bottles.

The refurbishments of 1988 are of the same architectural style as that of the Boulevard in Stonebow and feature bright brass fittings and tiled floors with a large stained-glass panel in the ceiling. The decor is finished off with a heavily embossed coving.

In 1986 the licensee, Andrew Knight, was captured by a raiding party from the Hansom Cab next door and held for ransom for £41, which was duly given to charity.

Meals are served every lunch-time while at night it becomes another of York's busy pubs.

Ye Olde Starre Inne

Stonegate   Grand Metropolitan   (map ref. No.46)

When the Parliamentarians, under the command of the Earls of Leven and Manchester and Lord Halifax, finally broke down the defences after the siege of York in 1644 the staunch Royalist, William Foster, was not too pleased at having to serve the Roundheads at his Inn, the Starre in Stonegate.

This well documented fact has allowed the Starre to maintain its claim as the oldest licensed Inn in York.

Another early landlord, Thomas Wyville, paid the princely sum of £250 for the Starre in 1662, when William Francis was the licensee.

Set back from the narrow Stonegate, the stables and yard have now been replaced by other tenements, leaving only a narrow entrance to York's most celebrated pub.

Because of the lack of main street frontage, the Starre advertises itself by the means of a beamed sign across Stonegate. One of the earliest references to the sign was in 1733 when the licensee, Thomas Bulman, agreed to pay George Ambler and John Moor 5s. yearly at Candlemas, to allow his sign to be fixed to their properties in Stonegate. Thomas Bulman, however, was a little craftier, as the agreement was that this sum could not be pocketed but had to be spent in the company of the said parties.

The Starre was a lot smaller than it is today and Cameron's Brewery spent £120,000 in 1985 on major refurbishments, yet still maintaining as much of the original character as possible.

A comprehensive range of home-cooked meals are served at lunch-time and early evening.

The York Arms

High Petergate   Samuel Smith's Brewery
(map ref. No.47)

Situated on the site of the ancient church prison of St. Peter, the York Arms was originally called the Chapter Coffee House, when in 1818 Ann Plowman was the licensee.

In 1838 this whole corner-block of segmented buildings was rebuilt to the design of J.P. Pritchett.

There appears to be a number of name changes from the 'Eclipse' in 1820/30 and then to the 'Board' in 1838 under the occupation of Thomas Cuthbert. This Board should not be confused with the other Board in High Petergate, which is now called the Hole in the Wall, as the latter did not become known as the Board until the 1950's.

By 1843 Thomas Cuthbert brought back the name Chapter Coffee House which remained until George Mitchell was listed as the licensee at the York Arms in 1861.

Consisting of two separate buildings the original pub has a small cosy bar to the front with another room to the rear. The left-hand side is now used for dining during the day and early evenings with a substantial variety of meals. The house speciality is giant-sized Yorkshire Puddings with a variety of fillings.

The Yorkshire Hussar

North St.   Cameron's Brewery   (Map ref. No.48)

The existing Yorkshire Hussar which was rebuilt in 1896 would appear to have become a public house when Thomas Birch Esq. of Warwick sold the property to Jane Fairfield for £450 in 1808.

For a period after this date it consisted of a butcher's shop and public house and was listed as the Yorkshire Tavern from 1843, when John Hanson was the licensee, until 1858 under the occupation of George Warrington. A year later the new licensee, Edward Holmes, lasted only a few months after he was fined 10s. for opening after time.

By 1889 the value of the property had risen to £900 when George William Carter purchased it. The licensee then was William Fowler.

On 3rd October 1930 the Yorkshire Hussar came under the ownership of the Spurriergate Brewers, John J. Hunt & Co. Ltd., who in turn were taken over by Camerons in 1958.

To the rear of the building are the remnants of the old stables with possible evidence of an earlier Sweet factory that produced 'Henry's Winter Nips'.

The Yorkshire Hussar is one of the few pubs where one can relax in the small bar without the 'rattle' of the inevitable 'bandit' or be deafened by the decibels of the juke box.

Lunch-time bar snacks are served through the week.